MILITARY VEHICLES
STRYKERS

BY JOHN HAMILTON

VISIT US AT
WWW.ABDOPUBLISHING.COM

Published by ABDO Publishing Company, 8000 West 78th Street, Suite 310, Edina, MN 55439. Copyright ©2012 by Abdo Consulting Group, Inc. International copyrights reserved in all countries. No part of this book may be reproduced in any form without written permission from the publisher. A&D Xtreme™ is a trademark and logo of ABDO Publishing Company.

Printed in the United States of America, North Mankato, Minnesota.
072011
092011

PRINTED ON RECYCLED PAPER

Editor: Sue Hamilton
Graphic Design: Sue Hamilton
Cover Design: John Hamilton
Cover Photo: U.S. Army
Interior Photos: Defense Video & Imagery Distribution System-pgs 6-7, 20-22, 24-25; Department of Defense-pgs 1-5, 12-15, 18-19, 29, 30-32; United States Air Force-pgs 26-27; United States Army-pgs 8-9, 11, 13, 16-17, 23 & 28.

Library of Congress Cataloging-in-Publication Data

Hamilton, John, 1959-
  Strykers / John Hamilton.
       p. cm. -- (Military vehicles)
  Includes index.
  Audience: Ages 8-15.
  ISBN 978-1-61783-078-5
1. Stryker armored vehicle--Juvenile literature. [1. Armored vehicles, Military. 2. Vehicles, Military.] I. Title.
  UG446.5.H2838 2012

TABLE OF CONTENTS

Strykers 4

Mission 6

Stryker Fast Facts 8

History 10

Versions 12

Wheels 14

Communications 16

Armor 18

Engine 20

Weapons 22

Transport 26

The Future 28

Glossary 30

Index 32

★STRYKERS★

Strykers are a family of United States Army infantry carrier and support vehicles. Strykers are fast and tough. With Stryker vehicles at their disposal, today's U.S. infantry can attack the enemy with speed and lethal force.

XTREME FACT

Strykers bridge the gap between heavy armor, like Abrams tanks, and light vehicles, like Humvees.

MISSION

Strykers were created to quickly and safely move soldiers to the battlefield. They rely on speed, stealth, and high-tech communications. Strykers are especially effective in urban settings. Troops can rapidly exit from the hydraulically lowered rear ramp.

A cavalry scout exits a Stryker vehicle in Iraq.

STRYKER FAST FACTS

Length:	22 feet, 11 inches (7 m)
Width:	8 feet, 11 inches (2.7 m)
Height:	8 feet, 8 inches (2.6 m)
Weight:	19 tons (19.2 metric tons)
Top Speed:	62 miles per hour (100 kph)
Cruising Range:	312 miles (502 km)
Crew:	2
Main Weapon:	M2 .50-caliber machine gun
Manufacturer:	General Dynamics Land Systems

HISTORY

After the Cold War ended in the early 1990s, the U.S. Army changed its focus. Modern warfare often demands armed forces that are flexible and can go anywhere in the world rapidly. Borrowing Swiss and Canadian designs, the Army developed a light, armored, eight-wheeled vehicle it called the Stryker. The first Strykers were sent to Iraq in 2003. They have also been used in Afghanistan.

Stuart S. Stryker

Medal of Honor

Robert F. Stryker

XTREME FACT

The Stryker is named after two unrelated American soldiers who posthumously received the Medal of Honor. Private First Class Stuart S. Stryker died in World War II. Specialist Robert F. Stryker died in the Vietnam War.

A Stryker arrives at Fort Irwin, California, in 2002.

VERSIONS

Strykers have two main versions. The Mobile Gun System (MGS) has a turret with a 105mm cannon to give troops direct fire support.

United States soldiers test fire a Stryker Mobile Gun System's 105mm cannon in Afghanistan.

Stryker Infantry Carrier Vehicle

The Infantry Carrier Vehicle (ICV) has a crew of two and can carry up to nine soldiers. It can be modified several ways. It can act as a reconnaissance vehicle, an anti-tank guided missile vehicle, or even as a medical evacuation vehicle.

The outside and inside of a Stryker medical evacuation vehicle.

WHEELS

Strykers have eight wheels. While not as rugged as the treads on a tank, wheels allow Strykers to move faster in urban areas. The eight-wheel design also allows the vehicles to maneuver very well over rough off-road terrain, including mud.

A soldier demonstrates the maneuverability of a Stryker as he speeds across wet pavement at Andrews Air Force Base in Maryland. The vehicle's tires are designed to move fast in urban areas.

XTREME FACT

Strykers use "runflat" tires, which are designed to function even if damaged by enemy fire.

COMMUNICATIONS

Strykers use sophisticated digital networks and computers to communicate with each other by radio, text message, or by battlefield positions on a real-time map. Unit commanders can mark enemy positions on a computer map, which are then instantly seen by other Strykers.

A soldier uses a *Stryker's* remote weapon system to scan an area for enemy contact during a 2007 training exercise in Australia.

ARMOR

Strykers protect their occupants from firearms and small explosions with a system of hard steel armor and lightweight ceramic and composite materials. Strykers can also be fitted with a cage of slat armor that encircles the vehicles, protecting them from rocket-propelled grenades.

A Stryker Infantry Carrier Vehicle (ICV) with a slat armor cage is positioned outside Mosul, Iraq.

The pressurized troop compartment in a Stryker vehicle protects soldiers against chemical and biological weapons, plus radiation hazards.

ENGINE

Strykers are powered by diesel engines manufactured by Caterpillar. Common parts with other Army medium-lift trucks makes maintenance easier. Many cables and hoses use quick-connect mechanisms. A Stryker engine can be completely removed and reinstalled in about two hours.

Military mechanics guide a Stryker's engine into a vehicle.

A combat repair mechanic replaces an exhaust fan in a Stryker vehicle.

WEAPONS

The basic Stryker Infantry Carrier Vehicle (ICV) is armed with an M2 .50-caliber machine gun. It can also be outfitted with grenade launchers or a 7.62mm M240 machine gun. Other Stryker variations are armed with 120mm mortars. Strykers are not designed to take on heavy armor such as tanks, but some are armed with TOW long-range anti-tank missiles to support infantry troops.

A Stryker armed with a machine gun and anti-tank guided missiles supporting ground troops in Iraq.

Soldiers test fire 120mm mortars from their Stryker Mortar Carrier Vehicle (MCV).

A TOW missile blasts out of a Stryker vehicle.

The Mobile Gun System (MGS) is a basic Stryker with a turret armed with a powerful 105mm cannon. It also has an M2 .50-caliber machine gun and two smoke grenade launchers. The MGS can fire its main cannon once every six seconds. The vehicle gives fire support to soldiers on the ground. It can directly attack enemy troops or hardened targets such as bunkers.

TRANSPORT

Strykers can be transported by ships or trucks, but they can also be rapidly delivered by airplanes. Strykers can fly in C-130, C-5, and C-17 cargo planes.

Strykers are loaded onto a C-5 Galaxy cargo plane for transportation.

AIR MOBILITY COMMAND

The Army boasts that it can put an entire Stryker brigade combat team anywhere in the world within four days.

Soldiers and their Stryker vehicles are transported aboard a C-17 Globemaster III.

THE FUTURE

The Army's 5th Stryker Brigade was deployed to the war in Afghanistan in 2009. A flaw in the Stryker's design became immediately apparent: the vehicle's flat bottom made it vulnerable to deadly mine blasts from below.

A Stryker lies on its side after an improvised explosive device (IED) exploded in the road under it.

In less than a year, the Army began deploying a new version: the Stryker Double "V" Hull (DVH). Its steeply sloped bottom is designed to deflect mine blasts up and away from the vehicle, protecting the troops inside. Several hundred Stryker DVH vehicles have already gone into service, with more on the way.

The 4th Stryker Brigade Combat Team, 2nd Infantry Division, made history as the last combat brigade to leave Iraq in August 2010. The soldiers and their Stryker vehicles moved to Kuwait.

GLOSSARY

ARMOR

A strong covering made to protect military vehicles.

BUNKER

An underground, protected shelter that is used to keep people safe.

DIESEL FUEL

A thick petroleum product that is used in diesel engines, such as those found in heavy tanks or trucks.

GRENADE

A bomb with a delayed explosion thrown by hand or shot from a rifle or launcher.

HULL

The main lower body of a heavy vehicle or ship.

INFANTRY

Soldiers who move and fight on foot.

MANEUVER

To move with skill to a specific location.

MEDAL OF HONOR
The highest military decoration awarded by the United States.

POSTHUMOUSLY
An honor that is awarded to someone after the person has died.

RECONNAISSANCE
To observe enemies to discover location, numbers of soldiers, weapons, and other key information to help with a strategic attack against them.

TURRET
The top part of a tank that houses the main cannon and other weapons. The turret rotates, allowing a gunner to aim and fire in any direction.

VIETNAM WAR
A conflict between the countries of North Vietnam and South Vietnam from 1955-1975. Communist North Vietnam was supported by China and the Soviet Union. The United States entered the war on the side of South Vietnam.

WORLD WAR II
A war that was fought from 1939 to 1945, involving countries around the world. The United States entered the war after Japan's bombing of the American naval base at Pearl Harbor, in Oahu, Hawaii, on December 7, 1941.

INDEX

A

Abrams tank 4
Afghanistan 10, 12, 28
Andrews Air Force Base
   14
Army, U.S. 4, 10, 20,
   28, 29
Australia 17

B

bunker 25

C

C-130 cargo plane 26
C-17 Globemaster III
   cargo plane 26, 27
C-5 Galaxy cargo plane
   26
California 11
Caterpillar 20
Cold War 10

D

Double "V" Hull (DVH)
   29

F

4th Stryker Brigade
   Combat Team 29
5th Stryker Brigade 28
Fort Irwin 11

G

General Dynamics Land
   Systems 9
grenades 18
grenade launcher 22,
   25

H

Humvee 4

I

improvised explosive
   device (IED) 28
infantry 4, 22
Infantry Carrier Vehicle
   (ICV) 13, 18, 22
Iraq 7, 10, 18, 22, 29

K

Kuwait 29

M

M2 .50-caliber machine
   gun 9, 22, 25
M240 machine gun 22
Maryland 14

Medical Evacuation
   Vehicle (MEV) 13
Medal of Honor 10
Mobile Gun System
   (MGS) 12, 25
Mortar Carrier Vehicle
   (MCV) 23
mortars 22, 23
Mosul, Iraq 18

R

remote weapon system
   17
runflat tires 15

S

2nd Infantry Division 29
slat armor 16, 18
Stryker, Robert F. 10
Stryker, Stuart S. 10

T

turret 12, 25
TOW missile 22, 23

U

United States 4

V

Vietnam War 10

W

World War II 10